# Writing Prompts –

# Random Words

*Learn what random word writing prompts are and how to use them*

*Written by Melissa Gijsbers*

# *Dedication*

To all the participants in Young Writers' Groups over the years who encouraged me to keep coming up with fun and creative writing activities.

# *Table of Contents*

# *Introduction*

Writing prompts can be a wonderful way to start a story, especially if you aren't quite sure where to start. There are many different sorts of prompts, and random word prompts are one of them.

With a random word prompt, you are given a number of words, I like to start with five although this could be any number, and then you use those words to inspire a story.

The challenge is to use all the words in your story in some way. If you want to mix things up, you can also add a theme such as Christmas or birthday to add an extra challenge.

This book will help you have fun with random word prompts, including showing some examples of how they can be used.

# *Word Lists*

Words for your stories can be found anywhere. You can pick some words at random, or use tools, like the magnetic poetry words, and pick out some words, ask others to suggest words, or even use a random word generator.

To help you, I have included a list of 100 words that you can copy and then print them out to pick out of a bowl or bag to get your words for your story.

With the random words, there is no right or wrong, they can be any words you like. Whenever I use them as a prompt, I aim to have them from different categories, for example, if I choose a colour, then I don't include another colour, same with animals, food, and so on. This provides variety and makes the challenge of coming up with a story a lot more fun.

One way to use the words below is to use a

random number generator and use that to choose the words.

| | | | |
|---|---|---|---|
| 1. | autumn | 14. | breakfast |
| 2. | baby | 15. | brother |
| 3. | bad | 16. | bus |
| 4. | ball | 17. | buying |
| 5. | bank | 18. | can |
| 6. | beach | 19. | car |
| 7. | bed | 20. | cat |
| 8. | bike | 21. | chalk |
| 9. | birthday | 22. | chocolate |
| 10. | biscuit | 23. | Christmas |
| 11. | black | 24. | cloud |
| 12. | blue | 25. | colour |
| 13. | board | 26. | crayon |

| 27. | dad | 43. | grandma |
|---|---|---|---|
| 28. | day | 44. | grandpa |
| 29. | delicious | 45. | green |
| 30. | dinner | 46. | happy |
| 31. | draw | 47. | hard |
| 32. | easter | 48. | hat |
| 33. | eat | 49. | help |
| 34. | fast | 50. | high |
| 35. | fence | 51. | home |
| 36. | flower | 52. | homework |
| 37. | foot | 53. | house |
| 38. | friend | 54. | hug |
| 39. | fruit | 55. | juice |
| 40. | fun | 56. | love |
| 41. | game | 57. | low |
| 42. | good | 58. | lunch |

| | | | |
|---|---|---|---|
| 59. | money | 75. | save |
| 60. | morning | 76. | school |
| 61. | mum | 77. | short |
| 62. | need | 78. | sister |
| 63. | night | 79. | slow |
| 64. | out | 80. | snow |
| 65. | owl | 81. | soft |
| 66. | party | 82. | spring |
| 67. | pink | 83. | summer |
| 68. | play | 84. | tall |
| 69. | please | 85. | teacher |
| 70. | potato | 86. | thanks |
| 71. | rain | 87. | thirsty |
| 72. | red | 88. | time |
| 73. | riding | 89. | today |
| 74. | sat | 90. | tomorrow |

| 91. | tree | 96. | winter |
|-----|------|-----|--------|
| 92. | umbrella | 97. | working |
| 93. | whale | 98. | yellow |
| 94. | wheel | 99. | yesterday |
| 95. | will | 100. | zoom |

# *Using the Words*

When you have your random words, think about how they can fit together to make a story. Sometimes it may be obvious, other times it may be a challenge; however, any challenge can be overcome with a bit of creativity.

Look at the words and think how you can use them.

You may want to use the words literally or be creative. If a word doesn't seem to fit, can you use it in another way. Can it be the name of a character or place or is there another way the word can be used?

With random word prompts, you can adjust the word slightly. For example, if the word is Sun, you could use Sunny, Sunshine, Suns, or similar and it still counts as you having used the word.

With the random word prompt, the challenge is to use the word at least once, so the word doesn't have to be an important part of the story.

The most important thing when writing your story is to have some fun with it and enjoy the challenge.

# Melissa's Golden Rules of Writing

Before I give you some examples of random word prompts and I have used them, here are my golden rules of writing:

1. **Have FUN!** - creative writing is all about the process. After all, if you're not having fun, what's the point?

2. **It's YOUR Story**—write your story your way. There is no single way to write a story, so experiment, play, and write whatever comes to mind.

3. **Experiment**—play with different styles and genre. You never know what you'll enjoy writing until you try. Plus, you don't have to limit yourself to just one type of writing.

4. **Try something new**—if your story isn't working, try something new. A different point of

view, style, genre, or even a new prompt if the one you're working on isn't working!

5. **Have FUN!** - Did I mention have fun? Whether you are writing something silly or serious, creating a story is fun, so enjoy it.

6. **Write as long or as short as you like**—If you only have a few minutes, then you can write something short. It doesn't matter if you don't finish a story or piece of writing in a sitting, or at all.

7. **First drafts are meant to be crappy***—this is something many people don't realise, it's no issue if your first draft is not perfect. Everything can be fixed up in the editing process.

8. **You don't have to finish**—if you're writing for fun, and you don't finish your story, that's okay. You can always come back and finish it another time.

9. **Have FUN!** - I may have mentioned this before… have fun writing your story, poem, or whatever else you're writing.

* Crappy = flawed, imperfect, incomplete, not up to scratch, unsatisfactory

# *Examples*

The following five stories are ones that I have written using random word prompts during writers' groups.

At the start, I will include the words I was given. When reading the stories, see if you can spot where the words were used and how I used them.

Afterwards, I encourage you to use those words and see what story you can come up with. And yes, we do like chocolate!

# Story 1 – Snow, Chocolate, Money, Green, Cat

The snow had stopped falling. Chocolate the cat curled up on his cushion in a sunbeam coming through the window.

'This is the life,' he thought.

Chocolate loved being a house cat. He was fed every day, had comfortable places to sleep, and a family of humans who adored him.

Out of the corner of his eye, Chocolate spotted some movement near the green armchair. He stretched and grudgingly went to investigate. Nothing was going to interrupt the serenity of his life, his home.

As quickly as he could, Chocolate went over to the place where he'd seen the movement. In the corner, trapped between the armchair and the wall, was a mouse. Once Chocolate appeared, the mouse started shaking.

'Please, Your Excellency. Don't hurt me,' squeaked the mouse in little more than a whisper. 'I didn't mean to come here, I got lost, and it's so warm in here.'

Chocolate eyed the obviously terrified mouse and tried to decide what to do next. Even though the snow had stopped, he knew it would still be freezing outside. Then again, the mouse had interrupted his nap.

'What's your name?' Chocolate asked.

'Money,' came the reply, 'Mum says it's because I have no sense.'

'Okay,' said Chocolate. 'How did you get inside?'

'There was a crack in the door,' said Money.

'The family don't like mice in here,' said Chocolate. 'They would want me to kill you.' Chocolate tried to look menacing. Money started to shake even more.

'Please, please your Amazingness,' squeaked Money, 'Don't kill me.'

Chocolate looked at the mouse. He knew what was expected, but the family wasn't around. Besides, chasing and killing mice wasn't his thing, and he had a nap to complete.

'Alright,' said Chocolate, 'I have a plan...'


Later that day, the family were surprised to see Chocolate curled up asleep on his pillow with a very realistic looking mouse toy. If they had looked a bit closer, they may have seen the mouse blink.

# Story 2 – Owl, Potato, Zoom, LOL

'Lol, lol,' Potato the owl sang from his position high in a tree. 'Lol, lol.'

'What on earth are you doing?' Mrs Possum called to Potato from her place in the hollow.

'I'm singing,' replied Potato, 'lol, lol.'

'That's not the right song,' said Mrs Possum. 'You're meant to hoot, that way my babies know it's time to get up. With you making that strange sound, they are still asleep.'

'But I was bored with singing hoot, hoot every night,' Potato said. 'I wanted to try something new. Lol, lol.'

'It's really not helpful,' said Mrs Possum. 'My kids should be awake now, zooming up and down the tree causing mischief. Instead, they are in bed, fast asleep until they hear their song.'

'I don't want to sing that song,' said Potato. 'This new one is fun. Lol, lol, lol.'

'Please, can you sing your old song,' Mrs Possum pleaded. 'Just for me?'

'Aren't you enjoying the peace and quiet?' Potato said. He really didn't want to change his song. Mrs Possum sighed.

'I was at first,' Mrs Possum admitted, 'But now I'm worried they won't go back to sleep in the morning.'

'Fine,' Potato said. He tried to hoot, but all that came out was lol. He cleared his throat and tried again. Still only a lol… 'Hang on a minute,' Potato said. He spread his wings and zoomed around the tree before settling on his branch again. He cleared his throat and began to sing.

'Hoot, hoot.'

The thing he heard was a scrambling in the tree, followed by the sight of baby possums zooming up and down, ready to cause mischief.

Potato wished he had stuck to his new song. He may have to find another tree.

# Story 3 – Chocolate, Bank, Working, Blue, Bed

'When I grow up, I'm going to work in a Chocolate Bank,' I rubbed my eyes.

'You what?'

'I will be working in a chocolate bank.'

That was a new one. It's not every day you're woken with your four-year-old jumping on your declaring their career choices.

'There's no such thing as a Chocolate Bank,' I said. It was Saturday, way too early to be awake, and freezing cold.

'Yes, there is,' she insisted, 'It's the place where Mummy's keep their chocolate so they don't have to hide it in the blue box on top of the fridge to hide it from Daddy's!'

I glanced at my husband, thankfully still fast asleep. I had thought my chocolate hiding place was a secret. I lifted up the corner of the doona for my daughter to snuggle in.

'Tell me more about this Chocolate Bank,' I said.

She started chatting away about the bank. As sleepy as I was, the more she spoke, the more a Chocolate Bank seemed like a good idea, especially the thought of depositing a cheap block of cooking chocolate that would turn into expensive, delicious chocolate over time. She had clearly been listening when her father explained the idea of putting money into a bank and the balance growing with interest.

Who knows, maybe there will be chocolate banks in the future. If anyone can do it, my four-year-old can.

# Story 4 – Autumn, Soft, Grandpa, Top Hat, Whale, Ferris Wheel

Note: For this one, the last three were emojis rather than words!

A day out with Grandpa was always an adventure, I never quite knew what to expect.

One autumn day, with the sun shining softly through the leaves on the trees, Grandpa and I walked hand in hand down a path. When we were away from the house, I started to hear music.

'What is it, Grandpa?' I asked.

'Sounds like a fair,' said Grandpa with a twinkle in his eye. 'Let's go, it could be fun.'

'Yes please,' I said.

We almost ran the rest of the way down the lane

before coming across the most amazing sight. In front of us was a fun fair! There were rides and side shows and the smell of all sorts of amazing food.

At the gate, we were welcomed by a man in a top hat.

'Roll up, roll up to Fabulous Freddie's Fun Fair. The Funnest Fun Fair in all the land. Today, and today only, everything is free!'

'Funnest isn't a real word,' I giggled.

'It is if you own a fun fair,' came the reply. 'Go and have some fun.'

'We will,' said Grandpa. 'What should we do first?'

'Ferris Wheel,' I said, 'that way we can look out over everything and plan our day.'

'Sounds good,' said Grandpa.

From the top of the Ferris wheel, we had a magnificent view of the fair. There was a big top for a circus show, side shows, pony rides, and just about anything else a kid could dream of.

We went to the side shows and won a stuffed whale. We ate fairy floss and hot dogs. Laughed at the clowns and were amazed at the circus show. Had a pony ride and dressed in Sumo suits for a fight.

As the sun went down, we started to walk home again.

I couldn't wait to show my stuffed whale to Mum and Dad and tell them all about the fair.

I wonder what our next adventure will be.

# *Story 5 – Homework, Fence, Love, Chocolate, Time*

That homework is better than chocolate. What a stupid topic for a debate. Everyone knows that nothing is worse than homework, and nothing is better than chocolate. I love chocolate, it's my favourite food of all time.

How am I supposed to convince anyone that homework is better than chocolate? I know I have 10 minutes for a speech, but what am I supposed to say? Pity I can't just sit on the fence, that's preferable to arguing in the affirmative.

There's all the stuff about needing homework to stay on top of your studies... but chocolate!

What about reducing sugar, obesity, and so on. I guess they are valid arguments... but chocolate!

I know that arguments to make, but how can I be convincing?

I think I need some chocolate to help me with this one...

# It's your turn

Now it's your turn.

Have a go with a random word prompt.

Find some words from one of the stories, the list provided, or another source and try to write a story of your own.

As well as the stories provided, here are some word collections you can use to get started:

1. Cat, fence, night, lunch, yesterday
2. Teacher, money, need, game, delicious
3. Ball, autumn, fast, help, party
4. Owl, friend, eat, Easter, draw
5. Morning, pink, riding, sat, thirsty
6. Potato, rain, snow, spring, tree
7. Please, love, green, hard, cloud
8. Christmas, hat, juice, save, thanks
9. Whale, today, low, homework, fruit
10. Happy, foot, black, baby, zoom
11. Yesterday, will, lunch, grandma, beach

12. Buying, can, eat, help, need

13. Day, car, fast, good, low

14. Bank, chalk, cloud, high, out

15. Love, game, black, car, working

16. Yesterday, thanks, soft, mum, help

17. Bed, day, grandpa, home, hug

18. Save, tall, umbrella, wheel, biscuit

19. Brother, fence, money, rain, red

20. Sister, school, umbrella, yellow, please

Remember, there is no single way to write a story, and you have my permission to write for the joy of it, to be there in the moment, and do things your way.

Write as if no one will read it and have fun.

# *About the Author*

Melissa Gijsbers is an author and booklover. Stories have always been a big part of her life and she has been writing them for as long as she can remember.

She started working with young writers in 2013 at the Monash Public Library and has been inspiring them to write by providing them with crazy writing prompts ever since! This group helped Melissa discover how important creative writing can be for wellbeing.

She currently lives in Gippsland in Victoria, Australia and spends quite a bit of time coming up with fun writing ideas for stories, as well as writing more books herself.

You can find out more about Melissa and her books on her website—
www.melissagijsbers.com

# *Also by Melissa Gijsbers:*

- My Princess Wears a Superhero Cape
- My Mummy is Evil
- Swallow Me, NOW!
- 3... 2... 1... Done!
- Lizzy's Dragon
- Genie in my Drink Bottle & other fun writing prompts
- Great Lost Sock Mystery & other writing prompts
- Creative Writing for Wellbeing

www.ingramcontent.com/pod-product-compliance
Lightning Source LLC
Chambersburg PA
CBHW072157020426
42334CB00018B/2056